HISTORY ALIVE THROUGH MUSIC

WESTWARD HO!

THE HEART OF THE OLD WEST

With
Illustrations From
AMERICAN HISTORY

Written By
DIANA WARING

Westward Ho! The Heart of the Old West
History Alive Through Music Series
by Diana Waring

© 1990 Hear & Learn Publications
ISBN 1-888306-25-4
(Previously published by Hear & Learn Publications, ISBN 1-879459-04-3)

Published by Full Quart Press
an imprint of Holly Hall Publications, Inc.
255 South Bridge Street
P.O. Box 254
Elkton, MD 21922-0254
Tel. (888) 669-4693

Send requests for information to the above address.

Cover design by Mark Dinsmore
Arkworks@aol.com

Cover illustration "The Rocky Mountains—Emigrants Crossing the Plains" lithograph 1866 by Currier & Ives
Courtesy of The Granger Collection, New York

Printed in the United States of America.

Thank You . . .

We would like to thank all who helped make this project a reality: Kim Waller and Luci Finley, who spent countless hours in research for the historic illustrations; Pamela DeWeese for her graphic design and typesetting; Randy Womack for his invaluable suggestions; Jim Evans, Mike Dickinson, Cliff Wood, Holly Kelly, and Lori Russell for their help with the vocals on the tape portion of this book/tape set; and Jodie Suckling, Lori Russell, Sue Standefer and Bill Waring who gave us their blessing in this venture.

Table of Contents

Introduction

"Westward Ho!" was the cry that stirred the hearts of thousands of Americans during the 1800's. Because of their brave and adventurous spirit, their ingenuity in overcoming great difficulties, and their desire to create a better life for their families, the American pioneer forged ahead to claim land all the way from the Atlantic Ocean to the Pacific.

Just imagine the difference in our country today if the area west of the Mississippi River all the way to the Rocky Mountains belonged to France (n'est ce pas?); Spain owned Texas, New Mexico and California (si, Señor); the people of Oregon and Washington were under British rule (Long live the Queen!); and, Alaska was Russian (Dasvydanya). Without the courage and determination of the American pioneer, our country would be largely unrecognizable today. We owe a great debt of gratitude to their memory.

"History Alive Through Music— Westward Ho!" is a sampling of times, places, and people of the Westward expansion. Some of the songs may be unfamiliar to you, but as you read the stories, study the pictures and listen to the music, it is our hope that the adventure, the danger, the dreams, the realities, the humor, the sorrow, the courage, and the faith of these Americans will come to life for you.   □

Craig, Diana, John, and Tad

Apple Picker's Reel

On December 1824, a British fur trading business called the Hudson's Bay Company, began building a trading fort on the Columbia River in the Oregon Territory. This fort, Fort Vancouver, became the primary trading center among all the Hudson's Bay Company forts in the Northwest, with warehouses built to store incoming goods and outgoing furs. Ships from England would bring to Fort Vancouver a year's supply of needed materials and equipment. The cargo included wrought iron and steel to be forged at the blacksmith shop, trade goods to be traded with the Indians and trappers for fur pelts, ready made clothing and fabric, mail, books and news of home, food supplies such as tea and coffee, and finally, new company employees. These company ships would then journey back to England laden with the valuable beaver pelts and other furs that had been traded throughout the past year. The furs were the lifeblood of the Hudson's Bay Company, their "raison d'etre" and the motivating force behind the exploration and establishment of forts in the Northwest. The fashion dictates of early nineteenth century civilization specified beaver felt as the epitome of style and culture for gentlemen's hats. As these hats were both unbelievably expensive and impressively longlasting, a man would carefully protect his purchase, eventually passing it down to his son or even his grandson!

In preparation for the outgoing voyage to the wilderness of the Pacific Northwest, it was the custom of the officers and employees of the Hudson's Bay Company to hold a farewell dinner in England. As legend records it, during one of these dinners held in 1825 or 1826, a young lady wrapped up seeds from the apple she was eating in a linen handkerchief, and presented this to one of the Hudson's Bay Company officers, Amelius Simpson. She said it was for the purpose of propagating this fruit in the Oregon Territory, though it was probably so he would remember the lass who had given them! He graciously promised to take the seeds, carefully placed them in his pocket,

and then promptly forgot all about them.

After seven or eight months at sea, including the treacherous trip around Cape Horn, Mr. Simpson arrived at Fort Vancouver. Seated one evening at dinner with Dr. John McLoughlin, the Chief Factor (another name for chief administrator), he reached into his pocket and found, to his surprise, the tiny present from England. He handed them over to Dr. McLoughlin, who received them joyously and carefully planted them with great watchfulness.

The immense success of those few apple seeds can be seen by the fact that when the first missionaries came to Fort Vancouver several years later, there was an abundant apple orchard under cultivation. In 1849, during the California Gold Rush, four bushels of apples from the Oregon Territory sold in San Francisco for $500! And today, Washington state is considered to be the apple capital of the world.

This song, Apple Picker's Reel, was written in 1966 by Larry Hanks (with the addition of verse three being written by the first grade class of Presidio Hill Elementary School). It has become a favorite of children all over the U.S. and Canada, but especially in the Pacific Northwest. As you listen and sing along with this merry tune, remember how the very first apples found their way to Fort Vancouver and realize how sometimes great things come from humble beginnings! □

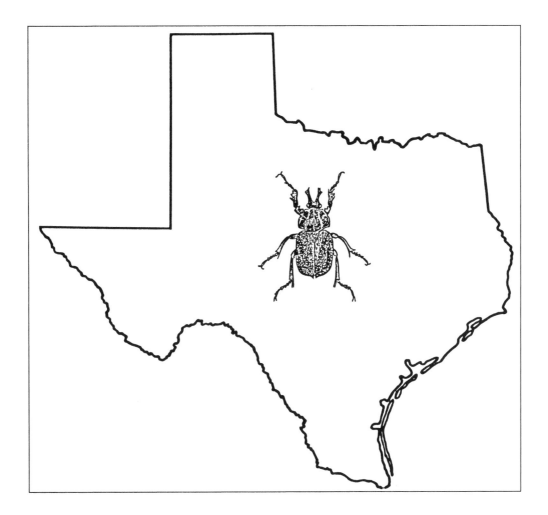

Boll Weevil

everal foreign nations including Great Britain, Spain, France and Russia had ruled over sections of North America from its discovery and exploration up to the nineteenth century. Spain was the first nation to lay claim to the land due to Christopher Columbus' discovery on behalf of the Spanish King Ferdinand and Queen Isabella.

The Spanish conquistadores brought to the New World the first horses and cattle, thereby introducing the elements that would forever change the American West. (Can you imagine hunting immense herds of buffalo on foot, or pulling a "prairie schooner" across the western U.S. without the benefit of oxen or horses?) Spain's colonialization extended from Mexico up into Texas, Arizona, New Mexico and California, by way of the Spanish priests in the Catholic missions. The missions were established for converting and training the Indians, but at the same time, for farming and raising cattle.

In 1821, Mexico declared independence from Spain, and required all persons in church leadership to take an oath against

Spain. The monks in Texas refused, turning over their missions to Indian converts and leaving much of Texas without any governmental protection for the Mexican settlers against the fierce Comanche tribes. This contributed favorably to the Mexican government's decision to allow American settlers to immigrate to Texas, thinking they could fend for themselves and perhaps discourage Indian attacks on all settlers. And once the invitation was given, the Americans came by the thousands! Whereas most of the land available in the expanding west was for sale at $1.25 an acre (with a minimum of 80 acres to buy), Texas was giving land away: 277 acres for farmers, or as much as 4,615 acres for those raising livestock along with farming the land.

Within ten years there were more than twenty thousand American settlers living in Texas, but relations with the Mexican government began to deteriorate as these Americans sought the opportunity for more autonomy and self-government. The situation became increasingly tense until by late 1835, the Texas Revolution had begun. Although the Americans suffered several defeats, including the Alamo and Goliad, they were able to catch their enemy literally sleeping, lulled by victory, in a surprise battle at San Jacinto on April 21, 1836. With Santa Ana, the head of the Mexican government, as their prisoner, the Americans were able to convince him that Texas should become a free republic. And so they won, fair and square, their independence from Mexico.

The Republic of Texas elected a president, Sam Houston, in 1836, and proceeded to try to join the Union. However,

because of Northern concerns in Congress that Texas would enter as a slave state (and had even engineered the revolution just to upset the delicate balance between North and South), it took nearly ten years for the Republic of Texas to become the State of Texas. Acceptance finally occurred on December 29, 1845.

Part of the developing culture of Texas revolved around the cattle industry (which will be seen later in the book), but Texas was also settled by farmers who brought some of their crops from the south when they immigrated. One of the chief cash crops of the south was cotton, and so, this lucrative crop became a vital part of the economy of Texas as well. The good Texas soil and climate produced cotton abundantly with few problems until 1892, when a tiny invasion of boll weevils crossed over the Rio Grande from Mexico. Within twenty years it rose from being an obscure bug to a catastrophic pest.

As we have seen before, one of the more popular responses to a difficult situation was to write a song which expresses not only the reality of the problem but the humor used to face it. Speaking of the Boll Weevil song (which was written around 1900), Carl Sandburg writes: ''A boll weevil couple, arriving in a cotton field in the springtime, will have, by the end of summer, more than twelve million descendants to carry on the family traditions.'' And as you might imagine, the favorite food of all twelve million descendants is the boll (or flower bud) of the cotton plant. Hence, the ongoing battle (raging even today) between determined farmer and hungry, prolific bug! □

Missonary's Farewell

On Thursday evening, February 18, 1836, a wedding was performed in Angelica, New York uniting Narcissa Prentiss and Dr. Marcus Whitman. The wedding was at the end of a congregational meeting of Narcissa's church and thus an audience and choir were present to witness these vows.

Prior to this, Marcus and Narcissa had each applied to the American Missions Board as missionaries to the Indians of the Oregon Territory. Since they planned to be married as soon as Marcus returned from his initial trip west, permission was granted for them to carry out medical work, evangelism, education and training among the Indians willing to allow them this privilege. Since time was of the essence in their journey to the west, plans were made to depart the day following their wedding.

After the vows were made and the sermon preached, everyone stood to sing the final hymn, Missionary's Farewell (written by Samuel Francis Smith, author of ''My Country 'Tis of Thee''). As they began to sing, emotion gripped the choir and little by little they were unable to continue. Only a few could sing with Narcissa, ''Yes,

I hasten gladly, From the scenes I love them well, Friends, connections happy country, Can I, can I say farewell . . .''

As they came to the last verse, the reality of the hymn was so powerful and the emotional response so strong that only Narcissa was able to continue and finish the song. With the sounds of sobbing as a background, she poured out the desire of her heart:

''In the desert let me labor
On the mountains let me tell
How He died — the blessed Savior
To redeem a world from hell!
Let me hasten, let me hasten,
Far in heathen lands to dwell . . .''

The next day the couple left on the start of their journey to the Oregon Territory. Narcissa was never to return.

They joined with another missionary couple, Henry and Eliza Spaulding in Cincinnati, Ohio, and made their way to St. Louis, Missouri to begin the actual trip west. They were able to travel much of the way in the company of a fur trading expedition which afforded greater safety and protection for the small group of missionaries. After traveling four long months, on the 4th of July, 1836, Narcissa Whitman and Eliza Spaulding crossed the Continental Divide, becoming the first white women to cross the Rocky Mountains. By September 12, they had reached Fort Vancouver (a welcome haven in the wilderness), proving that women could in fact, cross the continent and men need not leave their wives and children behind to come to the Oregon Territory.

Within a few months, the Whitmans had found a location for their mission, 25 miles north of Fort Walla Walla, on the Walla Walla River, among the Cayuse tribe. For eleven years they worked among the Cayuse, and also became an important resting point for the hundreds of American immigrants coming west on the Oregon Trail. Each year the number of Americans making this journey grew larger and larger, provoking animosity and fear among the Cayuse. But Marcus and Narcissa would turn no one away (including a family of seven children orphaned on the Trail who stayed permanently with the Whitmans).

The Immigration of 1847 had seen 4,000 people come across the Oregon Trail, bringing the population of American settlers to over 10,000. This was also the year that an epidemic of measles broke out, decimating many Indian tribes. Dr. Whitman was caring both for the sick American settlers and the sick Cayuse, working 'round the clock and traveling in all conditions. When many Americans lived and many Cayuse died, some of the Cayuse began to blame Dr. Whitman, even stirring up others by saying that he was trying to poison them so he might claim their lands for the white settlers. At last, on November 29, 1847, the emotional boiling pot of antagonism and fears overflowed. Marcus and Narcissa Whitman, two of their adopted children and ten others staying at the mission were massacred. The rest of the women, children and three men left alive were held hostage for a month until Peter Skene Ogden of the Hudson's Bay Company purchased their release.

Having been warned by various sources that the Cayuse were plotting their murders, Marcus and Narcissa evidently believed it worth the risk to stay and try to work out the difficulties and misunderstandings. The heartfelt desire expressed in ''Missionary's Farewell'' remained true for them until the end.

Oh California

n January 24, 1848, a small nugget of gold was found accidentally by James Marshall in the foothills of the Sierra Nevada Mountains. John Sutter, Marshall's employer, had been given a land grant in 1839 by the Mexican governor of California (California did not gain independence until 1848) to build a fort near the junction of the American and Sacramento rivers. By 1842 the fort contained a carpentry shop, a blacksmith, a tannery, gristmill and even a distillery. Sutter owned over 13,000 head of cattle and had much acreage planted in wheat and other grains. James Marshall had been hired to construct a sawmill forty miles

northeast of Sutter's Fort to provide lumber for this prosperous settlement. It was in the activity of building this sawmill that Marshall found gold. He reported this to his employer who urged him to keep quiet about the discovery. To his credit, Marshall did not tell anyone else, but as other employees found out and left their jobs to start digging, the news began to leak out. When word first reached San Francisco (then a sleepy little town on the coast of California), there was some doubt as to the validity of the reports. But in May, when miners came through San Francisco with large amounts of gold, gold fever struck with a vengeance. Almost everyone who could walk left for the gold fields, leaving behind a virtually deserted town. The rest of the country remained fairly ignorant of the proceedings in California until December 5, 1848, when President James K. Polk informed the nation in his annual message that large amounts of gold had been discovered in California. Almost overnight, a huge exodus of would-be miners began, and the business of getting them to California became "big business" indeed.

Folks living on the East Coast would generally go by way of sea to California while people living further inland found it much simpler to go overland by wagon train. As related in "Sweet Betsy from Pike" in History Alive Through Music — America, the trip overland was fraught with danger, difficulty and discouragement. On the face of it, people traveling by ship seemed to have a much easier route. But with the frantic posture of trying to be the first one to get to California, the ships' owners were converting every inch of space to passenger use with little thought for comfort or safety. Within six months of President Polk's announcement, most of America's ships, seaworthy and otherwise, had been pressed into passenger service between the East and California.

For those going by sea, there were two possible routes. One was to go all the way around the tip of South America, facing ferocious winds and tremendous gales at Cape Horn. The other was to sail to Central America, cross over to the Pacific at the Isthmus of Panama, and catch another ship to San Francisco. Unfortunately, even after the shortcut through the Panamanian jungle, the California-bound miners would face a long wait before the next ship would arrive (often several months).

Through all these hardships, willingly endured for the hoped-for prize, one song caught on as the theme song of these "Forty-niners." The tune was "Oh, Susanna," written by Stephen Foster, but the words were rewritten by one of the earliest Forty-niners, Jonathan Nichols of Salem, Massachusetts. He evidently wrote the words and then boarded the ship "Eliza" bound for the gold fields at the close of 1848. This "theme song," sung by those coming by sea on ships or overland by wagon reminded them, in the midst of frustration and difficulty, that for those who would "weather the storm," a pot of gold would be waiting.

Ho For California

Once these clerks, lawyers, teachers, doctors, tailors, mayors, blacksmiths, etc., reached the gold fields, they had to learn the fine art of digging and panning for gold. Usually they had to do back-breaking, bone-chilling work in order to find the small nuggets and gold flecks found in many of the claims. But there were some spectacular finds that gave hope that they too might find wealth beyond their wildest dreams.

In 1850, a nugget weighing twenty-five pounds was found in the North Yuba River, while the following year a twenty-eight pound lump of gold was found at the edge of a potato patch (talk about a "cash" crop). On the Feather River, a one hundred sixty-one pound boulder (!) of gold worth $38,000 was found and in 1854 the "grandaddy" nugget of them all was discovered. Weighing in at 195 pounds and valued at $43,534, it was found at Carson Hill by five miners discouraged by their inability to strike a gold vein. Another miner, George McKnight stubbed his toe one day while out looking for a stray cow. A piece of quartz broke off, and as he studied this toe-stubbing rock he discovered threads of gold within the quartz. The gold vein mined at that location has been worked since 1850, producing over eighty million dollars in gold!

However, for the vast majority of miners, the business of finding gold involved tons of sand and gravel, and was a tedious, physically demanding job. Since much of the gold was found along rivers and streams, many miners would work in the streambed as much as eight to ten hours a day in icy, mountain-fed water. This, along with the poison oak, smashed fingers and aching backs from hauling bucket after bucket of dirt, combined to make gold mining in the Sierra Nevadas an experience not soon forgotten (nor pleasantly remembered).

Some of the tools used to sort through the dirt for gold were the "washbowl" for panning, the cradle (or rocker) which would handle about one hundred bucketfuls of dirt per man per day, and, by 1851, the "long tom" which could process four hundred to five hundred bucketfuls of dirt per man per day.

The "washbowl" or goldpan, was the most portable of the three. A miner would scoop up half a panful of dirt on the banks of a stream along with plenty of water. Then gently swishing the water in a circular motion, he would slightly tip the pan so that some of the sand and water would spill out. He continued, adding water as necessary, until only the gold, which is several times heavier than the sand, remained in the bottom of the pan. Some gold panners never quite got the hang of it, so streams thought to be "panned out" often yielded, by other methods, gold that had slipped out of washbowls when no one was watching.

The cradle, which was much more efficient than a washbowl, was also a lot of hard work. The top was covered by an iron plate with holes in it. Dirt was shoveled

on this plate and the cradle was rocked, while water was poured over the dirt. Again, the heavier gold would settle to the bottom while the sand and water ran out. Operating a cradle did demand a certain amount of coordination—one miner likened it to patting one's head while rubbing one's stomach. (Imagine doing that eight to ten hours a day!) Miners needed to work cradles with at least one partner, which changed dramatically the solitary nature of gold mining.

The long-tom was a wooden trough, usually twelve to twenty-five feet long (although long-toms were constructed that were hundreds of feet long). A sheet of pierced iron was placed at the end of the trough with a collecting box underneath the sheet of iron. The long tom had to be set in a stream in such a way that water would run through it continuously, thereby making it usable only in certain locations. A miner would shovel dirt into the trough while his partner would pick out large stones and keep the rest of the dirt moving along. Again, the gold would drop through the holes in the iron sheet at the end of the trough while most of the sand would be washed away. Any remaining sand had to be separated out from the gold at the end of the day by panning.

It is interesting to consider that among the miners, few struck it rich and many lost everything they had invested, while those who provided services to the miners were able to earn much gold as payment. If these businessmen were careful to save their gold, they often ended up with enough to go back home and start a business. A few of the more notable of these who made fortunes from their California gold were John Studebaker (who went back to South Bend, Indiana and founded a company that made wagons and eventually, cars), Mark Hopkins (who became a founder of the Union Pacific Railroad) and Phillip Armour (who began a meat-packing plant in Chicago, Illinois). ☐

"Then Ho, brothers, Ho"
To California, go
There's plenty of gold in the world we're told,
On the banks of the Sacramento . . ."

San Juan Pig War

In the presidential election of 1844, the winning slogan of James K. Polk was "54-40 or fight!" This meant that all of the Oregon Territory which was jointly occupied by the U.S. and Great Britain should belong to the Americans. This was just part of an overall attitude of many Americans termed "manifest destiny" — that all of North America should be governed by the U.S. And so, President Polk first went to war with Mexico over the Texas boundary (and won!), then succeeded in gaining California for the Union and four weeks later forcefully negotiated with Great Britain for the Oregon Territory. Although, when the dust from all the rhetoric settled, the boundary was set at the 49th parallel.

In the midst of the excitement of all this acquisition of territory, one poorly worded boundary description in the Washington Treaty of 1846 almost resulted in war between Great Britain and the United States. The boundary between the U.S. and Canada was set at the 49th parallel, except for Vancouver Island where the Hudson's

Bay Company had built Fort Victoria as their new headquarters (after abandoning Fort Vancouver to the Americans). Unfortunately, the men drafting the treaty did not realize that within the geography of the area there were two passable channels separating Vancouver Island from the mainland. One of these channels, Haro Strait, lies west of a group of islands called the San Juans, while the other channel, Rosario Strait, lies east of these islands. The wording of the treaty simply draws the boundary line from ''the middle of the channel which separates the continent from Vancouver's Island . . .'' The question was, which channel?

For several years this issue seemed fairly insignificant to all concerned. In 1853, under the care of Charles Griffin, the Hudson's Bay Company landed 1300 sheep on San Juan Island because it was a very favorable place for raising sheep and other livestock. Everything remained fairly calm until 1859 when a few American settlers began setting up homesteads on this same island. The Americans had been told by American authorities on the mainland that the San Juan Islands would eventually be confirmed as belonging to the U.S., and in the meantime, the settlers had every right to settle there under the full protection of the American government.

Neither side was happy about sharing the island with ''foreigners'', and tensions began to noticeably increase. Keeping in mind that these islands were very inviting, with moderate climate, lush meadows and no natural predators, one can understand why both the Hudson's Bay Company and the Americans wanted very much to claim the land for themselves.

And now the stage is set for the high comedy of the San Juan Pig War. Enter Lyman Cutlar, a young Kentucky frontiersman with a reputation as a deadly shot. He settled on land one and one-half miles from the Hudson's Bay Company settlement, and commenced planting a half acre of potatoes. The Hudson's Bay Company livestock (including pigs) evidently developed a real taste for Cutlar's potatoes because he was constantly having to shoo them away. He made, on at least one occasion, formal complaint to Charles Griffin about a particularly large Hudson's Bay boar. Griffin's shouted reply was, ''It is your problem to keep your potatoes out of my pig!''

So it is probably no surprise to you that on the morning of June 15, 1859, Lyman Cutlar had had enough. Finding the boar munching on his little potatoes, smack in the middle of his potato patch, he grabbed his rifle, took aim and fired.

The song, ''The San Juan Pig War'', written in 1978 by John Dwyer, gives a pretty good picture of what happened next. The truly amazing part of this story is that the American and British soldiers, both quartered on this small island, never faced each other in battle. The crowning touch is to notice the year that this ''war'' was settled!

Chisholm Trail

In the year 1867, an enterprising young man named Joseph McCoy formulated a plan to attract Texas cattlemen and their herds of Longhorns to Abilene, Kansas. He planned to build a holding yard, or depot, for the Texas cattle going to eastern markets by rail. Cattle were in scarce supply in the East after the Civil War, and would sell for as much as $40-$50 per head, whereas in Texas, cattle were plentiful and could be had for as little as $4. With this kind of potential profit, many of the cattlemen began driving their herds north to meet the railroad, where the cattle could be easily shipped back East. Unfortunately, the Longhorns had been ''unwelcome guests'' in several states due to the Texas fever that broke out among the northern cattle after the Longhorns went through. It had become so bad that the Texas drovers (cowboys driving the cattle to market) were being stopped at gun point and told to find another way north. An alternative was to travel through the Indian Territory but often they would be required to pay a toll to the Indians for each head of cattle (and they might be stopped more than once to pay this toll!) Profits were going down and tempers were rising high about the time that McCoy opened his cattle depot. Abilene lay west of the American settlements (and the gun-toting farmers!), yet was far enough east to have access to the railroad.

McCoy built a holding yard that could contain up to 3,000 cattle at a time, a bank that could presumably contain all the profits and a hotel where the cattlemen could spend those profits. He then hired a friend to ride out, find all the herds of Longhorns being driven to market and inform the drover that Abilene was "a good safe place to drive to, where he could sell or ship his cattle" without any interference. By the end of that first season, 35,000 cattle had arrived in Abilene.

In order to encourage more business, McCoy printed up flyers describing the best route for the drovers to get to Abilene, took out ads in newspapers and even hired men to go and mark the trail from the Arkansas River to his depot. The trail from Texas to Abilene came to be known as the Chisholm Trail (named after Jesse Chisholm, a pioneer who blazed a portion of the trail prior to the cattle drives).

Evidently, Joseph McCoy's advertising campaign of the Chisholm Trail worked because the next year (1868) saw 75,000 Texas cattle come in to Abilene, 350,000 head in 1869, 350,000 again in 1870 and finally, 700,000 Longhorns driven north in 1871. That was the last year that McCoy's depot was used because of the growing number of gun-toting farmers settling in the area around Abilene. From that point, the cattle depots continued to move west of the settled areas. Many new frontier towns came into existence because of these depots.

"The Old Chisholm Trail," written in 1880, humorously reflects some of the adventures a cowboy would face in making this long trek to Abilene. But, at least from 1867 to 1871, he knew there was a dependable, friendly route by which he could bring his cattle to market, and that both he (with his paycheck) and his cattle (with their profit) would be welcome.

Westward Ho!

Mountain men . . . even today those words evoke a sense of mystery and a mystique of awe. These were the few intrepid, resourceful men who could live hundreds of miles from the closest white man, in potentially hostile Indian land, among grizzly bears who would kill them if given half a chance and without guaranteed supplies of food (you had to kill your dinner before you could eat it!). These solitary men, such as Jim Bridger, Kit Carson, Jedidiah Smith and Mike Fink were fearless in the face of danger, pursuing adventure and wealth by fur trapping in the vast wilderness of the West. It was these mountain men who discovered routes through the mountain ranges and watering holes on the plains. And as the fur trapping industry began to die down in the mid 1830's to 1840's, these were the knowledgeable and experienced guides that provided leadership to the first wagon trains heading to California and the Oregon Territory.

The early missionaries in the Willamette Valley of Oregon wrote letters home about the fertile soil, the mild climate and the price of land — 640 acres free! Eastern farmers whose soil had become depleted, growing little more than the rocks in the field, would hear of the new farming lands, sell out and hitch their wagons to join the increasing number of immigrants headed to ''The Promised Land.'' Under the watchful eye of the mountain men guides, these wagon trains would set off from Independence, Missouri, and begin their six-month trip across the vast wilderness.

At first the trip would be enjoyable, with a sense of camaraderie and fun prevailing among the immigrants. But after the first few weeks, the trail would become more arid, with the wagons churning up dust clouds that never quit 'till the wagons stopped in the evening. Also, fatigue would begin to set in from the incessant routine of the journey, beginning at four o'clock in the morning, walking eighteen miles in a day, caring for livestock, hunting for food and having too little time to rest. At the end of June they would reach Fort Laramie, less than one-third of the way to Oregon. As they would continue on their way to the Continental Divide, their guides would become relentless in keeping up the pace since they would know their group must beat the first snows in the passes or be trapped all winter on the wrong side of the mountain ranges. When at long last the wagon trains made it through the mountains (leaving behind family heirlooms, furniture, even food to lighten the loads), everyone would give a collective sigh of relief.

The guides eventually would make their way back to Independence to bring out another group of ''greenhorns,'' giving these wagontrains their best chance for survival. These mountain men were a breed apart from even the hardy pioneers who settled the west. Ever restless, exploring new regions, opening up vast territories to those who would come after, the mountain men were "bound for greater glory, Westward Ho!"

The verses to this song, "Westward Ho" are from an old poem written in the late 1800's. Tad Suckling, one of the partners of Hear & Learn, wrote the chorus and music in 1990, making it a musical picture reflecting the sentiments of the mountain men, trappers and guides in their quest for adventure and discovery. See if you can begin to understand what it was that separated these men from their peers and what compelled them on to new explorations as you listen to "Westward Ho."

Home On The Range

What was the "range" that the cowboys wrote of, dreamed of and sang about? It was the vast expanses of land used by the cattlemen for grazing their cattle. It was also the freedom a cowboy felt in roaming the prairies with his herds. In fact, the ability of the cowboys to graze their stock over the open range land was partly what gave rise to the huge herds in California, Texas, Wyoming and Montana. But it often provoked strained relations with neighboring farmers.

Laws influenced by Spain in the Southwest and Texas favored the cattlemen, requiring farmers in the area to take responsibility for protecting their own crops and orchards with fencing. The laws brought over from Britain to the eastern U.S. favored the farmers by placing the burden of responsibility of protecting crops on the cattlemen's shoulders. As the western part of the country drew thousands upon thousands of Eastern settlers, legislators were elected who established laws which protected the rights of the farmers.

As a result, cattlemen were forced to hire cowboys to "ride the ranges," keeping their cattle from trespassing on others' property. These range riders would have to ride the "lines" separating their cattle from those on the other side, or from a settler's land. As one line rider wrote. "It is not hard work, but decidedly monotonous, riding by yourself for so many hours every day. A good line-rider ought to be able to see if any cattle have left the range by the tracks they leave on the ground as they pass out, and must then follow up the trail and bring them back. The chief difficulty I always found was to distinguish between the old and the fresh trails, unless there had been sufficient rain to wash out the old tracks.'' The line riders lived in line shacks and would only see another person when the chuck wagon would bring up more supplies, or they'd run into another rider. Obviously, this was not a job for socialites.

Barbed wire and its use as cheap fencing brought about even more changes for the cattlemen accustomed to open ranges. As people began settling the open ranges and fencing in their land, trail drives to the north became increasingly difficult, with little grazing land left to feed the moving herds. One Texas trail driver summed up the attitudes of many cattlemen when he wrote, ''Fences, sir, are the curse of the country.'' Invented in 1873, barbed wire took a few years and some pretty fancy sales pitches to catch on, but, as it gained in popularity, it changed the open range cowboy culture forever.

''Home on the Range,'' written in 1873, suggests some of the pleasure cowboys found in riding the open range before barbed wire fences made their mark. Progress and the settlement of the Midwest was indeed encouraged because of that invention, but it caused a whole way of life, one of the most romantic and colorful in American history, to quietly end.

Little Old Sod Shanty

n 1862, Congress passed a law which had been the subject of national debate for twenty years. This bill, known as the Homestead Act, enabled anyone who was at least twenty-one years of age, the head of a family, and a citizen (or hoped-to-be citizen) of the U.S. to claim 160 acres of public land, if they agreed to live on that land for five years and make improvements. The privilege of free homesteading had been greatly sought by the nation's early farmers, but the newly-formed government had supported itself by selling public land. They felt they could not afford to give it away. Eventually, the real question of free homestead land boiled down to a question of the slavery issue: would a newly settled territory filled with homesteading farmers come into the Union for or against slavery? The South would take no chances and voted down the homesteading bill whenever it came up. However, in 1862, with the Civil War raging in the background and the southern votes stilled by their absence, the

Homestead Act passed into law.

Advertisements of the unbelievably good offer of 160 acres of land free were made throughout this country and Europe, attracting as many as half a million families to the West. As California, Oregon and the Washington Territory became increasingly settled, the hearts of the adventurous turned to the mid-west which some had formerly known as the "Great American Desert"! It is now called the Great Plains and includes eastern Montana, Wyoming, Colorado, New Mexico, western North Dakota, South Dakota, Nebraska, Kansas, Oklahoma and Texas.

There were many adventures awaiting those courageous enough to settle and farm the Great Plains. Facing constant danger from the fierce Plains Indians, they were handicapped by their "long rifles" which could not be used on horseback. Water for crops and livestock was dependent on fickle spring and summer rains until the introduction of the windmill in the 1870's. Fencing was non-existent on the treeless plains until the invention of barbed wire in 1873. And with no lumber (only a few scraggly trees), houses had to be constructed from what was available—dirt and sod.

To build these houses of sod, the pioneers would cut strips of the prairie into one-foot blocks, then stack these blocks into walls. The roof would usually be sod blocks or thatch, supported by wood brought from the East or branches scrounged from the area. The good news was that these sod shanties were warm in winter and cool in summer, but the bad news was the occasional bits of dirt falling into the food and the uninvited critters, such as rats, mice, snakes and gophers, who also took up residence.

"Little Old Sod Shanty," written around 1870, provides us an opportunity to peek inside and understand the realities of day-to-day living for these Plains settlers, and to know what motivated and inspired them in their task of transforming the wilderness. In spite of loneliness and hardship, this settler concludes that . . . "I wouldn't trade the freedom that I have out in the West, for the table of the eastern man's own home." □

Strawberry Roan

fter the Civil War, American writers captivated their audiences by fanciful tales of the rugged, range-riding cowboy of the west. Although herding cattle on horseback had been an occupation for hundreds of years, it was the mystique of long trail rides, herding thousands of cattle to northern markets that captured the imagination of our war-weary country. Suddenly, dime novels with ''bigger-than-life'' stories about the cowboy sprang into popularity. The ranks of cowboys from Texas swelled with the addition of boys and young men from back east who wanted to live the life they'd read about. Most lasted a year or less due to the dissimilarity be-

tween fiction and real life, but others would quickly take their place.

What did the cowboys really do? After the invention of barbed wire, there was little need for line riders, except to occasionally ride along this new-fangled fence, checking to see if it was holding up to its' reputation. In the spring, cowboys would gather up the newborn calves with their mothers and make sure they were in good, green pasture. The cowboys also would ride the range looking for sick or injured cattle. If they found any unbranded calves, they would brand them on the spot to prevent their being ''rustled'' by cattle thieves. (It's downright difficult to prove ownership without a brand.) But one task was common to all cowboys: breaking wild horses. Regardless of what the Hollywood movies depict, there was no easy way to get this job done.

The first step in breaking a wild horse is to catch it, which is easier written than accomplished! Will James, the famous cowboy artist, wrote, "Most any bronc is a ticklish proposition to handle when first caught . . . It's not always meanness, it's fear of the human. They only try to protect themselves." In the process of "protecting" himself, a horse can cause considerable consternation to the cowboy. And whether a cowboy would use gentle methods of persuasion or the "go for the gusto" approach, riding a wild, bucking bronco was a bone-janglin', hair-raisin', blood-pumpin' experience. Even so, most cowboys preferred

their "tamed" mounts to buck a little first thing in the morning (better than a cup of coffee for waking up a sleepy cowboy!). According to Will James, "I figger it's their mettle showing when they do . . . I've seen and rode many a good old well-broke cow horse what had to have his buck out in the cold mornings, just to kind of warm hisself up on the subject and settle down for the work ahead."

Not all horses were agreeable enough to allow themselves to be broken, thus providing many entertaining hours of combat for the cowboy.

"Strawberry Roan," written sometime between 1870 and 1890, gives a classic example of this contest between cowboy and wild "cowboy-breakin' " bronc. Today this form of entertainment is called "Rodeo!"

□

Old Settler

American settlers coming across the Oregon Trail in the 1840's were strongly encouraged by the employees of the Hudson's Bay Company to live south of the Columbia River. These employees were British, and Great Britain intended that river to be the dividing boundary line between the U.S. and Canada. However, when the boundary question was settled in 1846, the line was drawn about 300 miles to the north, leaving most of Puget Sound free for American settlement. There was very little open land for farming in this area due to the dense forests but with the 1848 discovery of gold at Sutter's mill, lumber shipments for the gold fields became an important and profitable source of income. The earliest settlers began writing letters back east to tell friends and family about the abundance of food, the pleasant climate and the ready-at-hand lumber market on the shores of Puget Sound.

In this song, Old Settler, written in 1874 by Francis Henry, we have a tongue-in-cheek glimpse at a man disillusioned by the gold fields heading north to try his hand at farming in the Puget Sound area of the Pacific Northwest. Evidently no one told him of the dense forest to be cut down before he could begin the business of farming, but he eventually acclimated and found the abundance of the region to be a veritable Garden of Eden.

What did the pioneer of the mid 1880's face on this journey to Puget Sound? Generally, once they crossed the Rocky Mountains they would travel to the Columbia River, then downriver to Fort Vancouver. From this point the pioneers would travel north until reaching their new homestead. However, in 1853, a small group decided to head due west from Fort Walla Walla through the Naches Pass in the Cascade Mountains. Though this route would save over 200 miles, they found it almost impossible, crossing one curving river more than 60 times!, traveling through sagebrush as tall as the wagons, finding no grass for the oxen for fifty miles, running low on food for themselves, having to fell trees to make a path as they started up through the mountains, and finally coming to a "jumping off place" — a sheer thirty foot bluff with a steep slope beyond that. The travelers had a rope 180 feet long but it wasn't long enough to get them down the jumping off place to the floor of the valley below, so four oxen were killed and their hides were cut into strips to tie to the rope. With this system they lowered the wagons over the edge, only losing two out of thirty-six. After this remarkable feat they were met by settlers from Puget Sound and Hudson's Bay Company men who provided them with enough food that starvation was no longer a danger. The following year a rugged but passable road was forged through the

mountains and forests so that succeeding groups of pioneers would have a somewhat easier time of it.

There were dangers, difficulties and isolation once you had arrived in the Pacific Northwest, but in spite of all of these, life here seemed good for the old settlers. There was always plenty of wood for the fire and it would be hard to go hungry if you lived close to Puget Sound. In fact, early settlers had a saying about the food available from the tidelands, "when the tide is out, the table is set!" All you needed was a shovel and a bucket, and soon there would be a feast . . .

"Surrounded by acres of clams . . . I think of my pleasant condition, surrounded by acres of clams." □

GOUIE DUCKS

Gooey Duck

O ur pioneer forefathers and mothers spent a majority of their lives providing food for their families. Whether it was hunting and fishing, gathering berries and roots, or cultivating gardens and raising chickens, this business of ''keeping body and soul together'' was seriously pursued.

As the people from the East began their trek to the West, they provisioned themselves with bacon, flour, salt, sugar, coffee and little else. On their journey, they became so bored with the unvarying menu that if the opportunity presented itself, the immigrants jumped at the chance to sam-

ple new and unusual foods, such as buffalo, for instance. This was quite a providential preparation considering some of the unique natural resources awaiting them at the end of their trip.

In the Puget Sound area of the Pacific Northwest, early settlers were severely limited in their normal course of fare. Because food stuffs from back East had to go around Cape Horn, the cost of even flour was prohibitive to many. So they planted their precious vegetable and grain seeds and waited for harvest, eating in the meantime what the Indians ate: fish, berries, wapatoes (Indian potatoes), roots, birds and game. One of the most bountiful resources for Indians and settlers alike was found in the waters of the Northwest. Salmon, steelhead and trout were found in the rivers, and shellfish (oysters, clams, mussels, crab) on the tideflats of Puget Sound. There were many varieties of shellfish but the prize for the biggest goes to the geoduck (pronounced "gooey duck"). Weighing ten pounds (!), these long necked clams could only be found at the lowest tides, but even one would make enough clam chowder to feed a BIG family. Despite their generous size and the relative ease in digging them, many people refused to eat geoducks because they were so ugly. Look at the picture and see if you agree!

After the settlers established themselves on their plot of land, they began improving the surrounding countryside with roads, bridges, schools, meeting halls, churches and eventually, industries. Puget Sound had many industries devoted to the natural resources of the area such as logging, mining and fishing. Even the lowly geoduck was harvested commercially in the early 1900's until clam diggers noticed the depleting numbers at lowtide. Fearing they would become extinct, people passed laws prohibiting commercial digging of these giant diminishing clams. The geoduck, however, had one more claim to commercial fame. In the 1950's, U.S. Navy divers working in the Puget Sound waters noticed huge numbers of long necked clams in extremely deep water. These indeed proved to be geoducks, which were now understood to be true deep-water clams, found at depths of as much as 360 feet!

Commercial harvesting was allowed to begin again in 1970 in water that is at least one-quarter mile from high tide. Today, these harvesters take out between three to five million pounds of geoduck each year, and most of it is consumed in the U.S.!

To the delight (and financial gain) of the geoduck harvesting industry, a catchy song about these winsome creatures was written in 1972 by Ron Konzak. It was an immediate hit in the Pacific Northwest, as well as in Japan and Australia. It also helped to boost sales of this edible — as long as you don't look at him — geoduck. □

Little Cabin In
The Cascade Mountains

 t seems fitting, somehow, to end our westward adventure with a song that expresses the sheer contentment of having found what many pioneers were seeking.

This song, "Little Cabin in the Cascade Mountains," written in 1929, was the last song composed by Harold Weeks. He was among the first and most famous composers from Seattle who wrote songs that were nationally popular (he co-authored ''Hindustan''). This song from the end of his career summed up his vision of the ''good life.''

widely separated by our holdings of three hundred and twenty acres of land to each family. In those days anyone residing within twenty miles was considered a neighbor; and we soon became united in love and

> *''There's a little cabin in the Cascade Mountains*
> *that is where I want to be,*
> *Where the tall trees frown, and the streams*
> *come tumbling down and the trout leap lustily,*
> *Where the hills lay hazy in the sunshine lazy*
> *and the day ends peacefully,*
> *Oh that little cabin in the Cascade Mountains*
> *is a paradise to me.''*

Another resident of what was first ''Oregon Territory,'' then ''Washington Territory,'' and finally, in 1889, Washington State, was a pioneer woman by the name of Phoebe Goodell Judson. In 1853, she and her husband traveled by wagon from Ohio, across the Oregon Trail to the Puget Sound area. In her memoirs of this trip and subsequent adventures, entitled ''A Pioneer's Search for an Ideal Home,'' Mrs. Judson describes the various places they lived, people they met and experiences they faced before finally settling in the northwest corner of Washington. Of the first place they settled, Grand Mound, she writes of the families (including her own parents) who claimed land close by. This excerpt is included for the way it communicates the sentiments of the pioneers who made their home in the wilderness:

''We were now all told, eleven families within a radius of six or eight miles,

sympathy, for it was not riches, splendor, fame or glory we were seeking, but happiness, peace and contentment, while each was bearing the privations incident to a pioneer's life, and doing his part in helping to develop a new country. Our wants and cares were few, for our simple style of living corresponded with the primitive environments of the territory . . . Our earthly possessions now consisted of one yoke of oxen, wagon, cow and calf, and a squatters' right to three hundred and twenty acres of wild land, enriched with an unlimited supply of gravel — and we began to consider ourselves quite ''plutocratic.''

''Had an aristocrat called upon us, we would have invited him to repose in the cozy depths of our fine upholstered three-legged reception stools, by the side of the glowing flames in our mud tiled fireplace. But there were none of that class to call . . . 'Twas not the pretentious millionaire or magnate controlling the finances of the world who invaded these quiet domains, but the hospitable, whole-souled homeseekers were the first who ventured to penetrate the solitude of this wild, picturesque country of "never fading green," and they are the ones who lived the most happy, useful lives while toiling to develop its many resources."

"Little Cabin in the Cascade Mountains" is our musical conclusion to this look at the western expansion of the U.S.A. Many people lost their lives in the journey west, most left beloved family and friends in the East in order to build a better life for themselves and their children, and all worked harder than we can, today, even possibly imagine to settle an untamed wilderness. As Phoebe Judson concludes: "After all the trials and hardships that have been our lot while journeying through the wilderness, I would not exchange my "buried" life, as it has been called, for the "wear and tear" of the fashionable society woman who must fulfill her social obligations, with no fruit to show as the result of her hard labor." Seeing how these formidable settlers impacted the western half of the United States (the long-term fruit of their labor), we can truly say that this is a happy ending!   ☐

Epilogue

One of the benefits of studying history is to learn from the failures and successes of our forefathers. What do you think provided the most long lasting satisfaction, contentment and happiness for these pioneers of the West? Consider the gold seekers of 1849. What was their probability of finding what they sought? What about the young men from the East who came to Texas to pursue their dreams of fame and adventure as cowboys?

What about the homesteaders seeking to carve out a home in the wilderness? Finally, look back through these songs and stories and decide which of these people were the most content and satisfied with their lives. What do they have in common? What conclusions can you make? And how will these lessons of history affect your own life? ☐

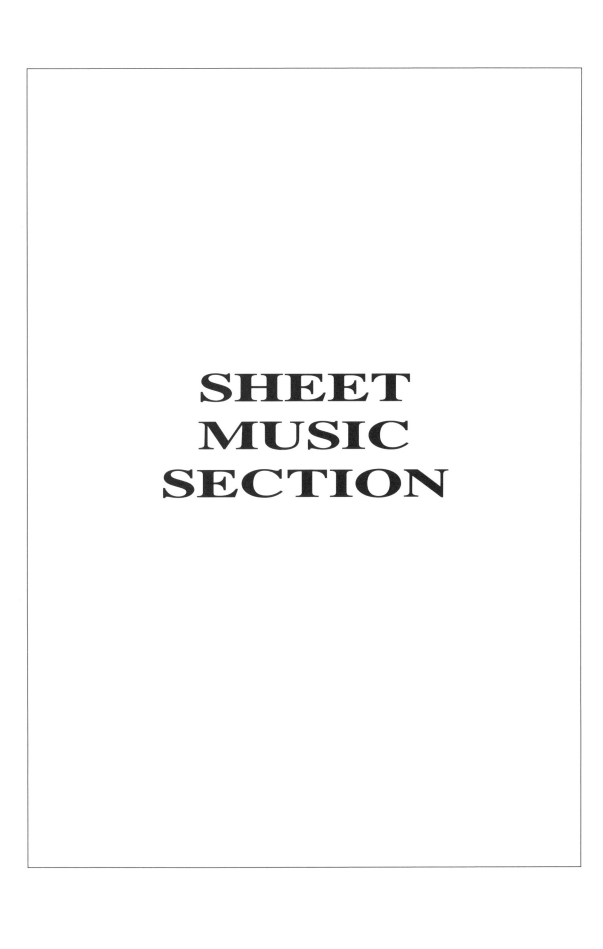

SHEET
MUSIC
SECTION

Apple Picker's Reel

Words and Music by
Larry Hanks

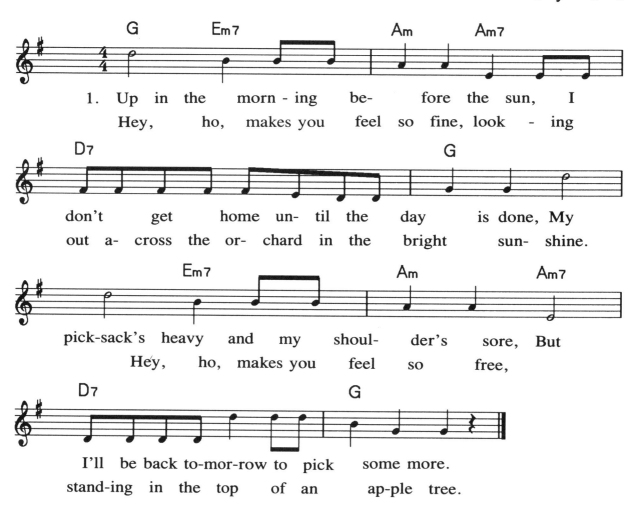

1. Up in the morn - ing be- fore the sun, I
Hey, ho, makes you feel so fine, look - ing

don't get home un- til the day is done, My
out a- cross the or- chard in the bright sun- shine.

pick-sack's heavy and my shoul- der's sore, But
Hey, ho, makes you feel so free,

I'll be back to-mor-row to pick some more.
stand-ing in the top of an ap-ple tree.

Apple Picker's Reel

CHORUS
Start at the bottom and you pick 'em from the ground,
And you pick that tree clean all the way around,
Then you set up your ladder and you climb up high,
And you're looking through the leaves at the clear blue sky.

FIRST CHORUS
Well, they come in yellow and green and red,
And you eat 'em in the mornin' and before you go to bed,
You can play catch if you throw 'em up high,
Whoops! Squish! Apple pie!

FINAL CHORUS
Hey, ho, you lose your mind,
If you sing this song about a hundred times,
Hey, ho, you feel so free,
Standing in the top of an apple tree.

The Boll Weevil

Cowboy

The boll wee- vil is a lit- tle black bug from

Mex-i-co they say, Came all the way to Tex-as, Just a-

look- ing for a place to stay, Just a- look- ing for a

home

(Just a- look- ing for a home).

Just a- look- ing for a

home.

(Just a - look - ing for a home).

The Boll Weevil

The first time I saw the boll weevil he was sitting on the square,
The next time I saw that boll weevil he had all his family there,
Just a-looking for a home, etc.

The farmer took the boll weevil and stuck him in hot sand,
The weevil told the farmer, ''I am going to stand it like a man
'Cause it's going to be my home,'' etc.

The farmer then took the bollweevil and stuck him on a cake of ice,
The weevil told the farmer, ''This is mighty cool and nice,
And it's going to be my home,'' etc.

The merchant got half the cotton, and the boll weevil took the rest,
He only left the farmer just a single old ragged vest,
He had found himself a home, etc.

Missionary's Farewell

Words by Rev. Samuel F. Smith
Tune: Traditional

1. Yes, my na- tive land, I love thee; All thy
Friends, con- nections, hap- py country, Can I

scenes I love them well; Can I leave thee, can I
bid you all fare- well!

leave thee, Far in heath-en lands to dwell? Can I

leave thee, can I leave thee, Far in heath-en

lands to dwell?

Missionary's Farewell

Home! — thy joys are passing lovely —
Joys no stranger-heart can tell;
Happy home! — 'tis sure I love thee!
Can I — can I say — Farewell?

CHORUS
Yes! I hasten gladly,
From the scenes I love so well;
Far away, ye billows bear me;
Lovely native land! — Farewell!

SECOND CHORUS
Pleased I leave thee, pleased I leave thee,
Far in heathen lands to dwell.
Pleased I leave thee, pleased I leave thee,
Far in heathen lands to dwell.

In the deserts let me labor,
On the mountains let me tell,
How he died — the blessed Saviour
To redeem a world from hell!

THIRD CHORUS
Let me hasten, let me hasten,
Far in heathen lands to dwell.
Let me hasten, let me hasten,
Far in heathen lands to dwell.

Oh, California

Music by Stephen Foster
Words by J. Nichols

I came from Sa- lem Cit-y, With my wash-bowl on my

knee, I'm go-ing to Cal-i- for-nia, The gold-dust for to

see, It rained all night the day I left, The wea- ther it was

dry, The sun so hot I froze to death Oh, bro-thers, don't you

cry! Oh, Cal-i- for-nia, That's the land for me! I'm

bound for San Fran- cis-co With my wash-bowl on my knee.

Oh, California

I jumped aboard the 'Liza ship
And traveled on the sea,
And every time I thought of home
I wished it wasn't me!
The vessel reared like any horse
That had of oats a wealth;
I found it wouldn't throw me, so
I thought I'd throw myself!

CHORUS
Oh, California, that's the land for me!
I'm bound for San Francisco with my washbowl on my knee.

I thought of all the pleasant times
We've had together here,
I thought I ought to cry a bit,
But couldn't find a tear.
The pilot's bread was in my mouth,
The gold dust in my eye,
And though I'm going far away,
Dear brothers don't you cry!

CHORUS

I soon shall be in Frisco,
And there I'll look around,
And when I see the gold lumps there
I'll pick them off the ground.
I'll scrape the mountains clean, my boys,
I'll drain the rivers dry,
A pocketful of rocks bring home
So brothers don't you cry!

CHORUS (2 times)

Ho! For California

D.D. Emmett & J. Hutchinson

We've formed our band and are well mann'd, To jour-ney a-far to the pro-mised land, Where the gold-en ore is rich in store, On the banks of the Sac- ra- men-to shore. Then, ho! Bro- thers ho! To Cal-i-for- nia go. There's plen-ty of gold in the world we're told, On the banks of the Sac-ra- ment-o. Heigh ho, and a- way we go, Dig- ging up gold in Fran- cis co.

Ho! For California

O! don't you cry, nor heave a sigh,
For we'll all come back again, bye and bye,
Don't breathe a fear, nor shed a tear,
But patiently wait for about two year.

CHORUS
Then, ho! brothers ho! to California go.
There's plenty of gold in the world we're told,
On the banks of the Sacramento.
Heigh ho, and away we go,
Digging up gold in Francisco.

As the gold is thar, most any whar,
And they dig it out with an iron bar,
And where 'tis thick, with a spade or pick,
They can take out lumps as heavy as brick.

CHORUS

As we explore that distant shore, —
We'll find our pockets with the shining ore;
And how 'twill sound, as the word goes round,
Of our picking up gold by the dozen pound.

CHORUS

We expect our share of the coarsest fare,
And sometimes to sleep in the open air,
Upon the cold ground we shall all sleep sound
Except when the wolves are howling round.

CHORUS

As off we roam over the dark sea foam,
We'll never forget our friends at home
For memories kind will bring to mind
The thoughts of those we leave behind.

CHORUS

In the days of old, the Prophets told
Of the City to come, all framed in gold,
Peradventure they foresaw the day,
Now dawning in California.

CHORUS

O! the land we'll save, for the bold and brave—
Have determined there never shall breathe a slave;
Let foes recoil, for the sons of toil
Shall make California GOD'S FREE SOIL.

FINAL CHORUS
Then, ho! Brothers ho! to California go,
No slave shall toil on God's Free Soil,
On the banks of the Sacramento.
Heigh ho, and away we go,
Chanting our songs of freedom, O.

San Juan Pig

Words and music by
John Dwyer

1. Let me tell you of a sto-ry of a
2. Now the pig it was Ca-na-di-an, the

San Juan pig. It wasn't worth much 'cause it
settler was a Yank. What the pig did to his gar-den was

was-n't ver-y big, But it root-ed in a gar-den and it
more than just a prank, For it dug up his po-ta-toes and it

near-ly caused a fray, Be-
tore down his fence, Since it

tween the King of Eng-land and the U.– S.–
was-n't just the first time Cut-ler's anger was im-

A.
mense.

San Juan Pig

When he saw the pig a-rootin', Lyman Cutler, he got sore.
He grabbed up his musket, for the pig he tore.
The pig saw him comin' and headed for the woods,
But he stopped at the edge, and Cutler shot him good.

Then Cutler felt regretful and went down to Hudson's Bay,
And told the clerk in charge of the porker he would pay.
Griffin said, ''One hundred dollars, he's a prize breeding boar.''
Cutler told him 'I'll pay three, and not a penny more.'

Then up stepped A.G. Dallas, and said, ''See here, my man,
You're already trespassing upon Canadian land.
You know it's British country from Rosario to the west,''
''Not so, '' said Lyman Cutler, ''East of Haro is U.S.''

Well, the settlers they backed Cutler with their muskets in their hands.
The British thought is wiser not to make a stand.
The stars and stripes were hoisted to celebrate the day,
And were seen by General Harney a'sailin' on the bay.

The general came ashore and he listened to their tale.
He was a man of action and to help he did not fail.
To Fort Bellingham he sent 'ere he sailed away again,
And down came Captain Pickett with a company of men.

Then up sailed the British with war ships one, two, three,
Which made a few too many for Pickett's company.
They had to find a way to even up the score,
So he sent to Fort Steilacoom and got five hundred more.

Well they argued in the Senate, and in the House of Lords,
And they didn't make much progress but they used a lot of words.
So they asked the German Emperor the boundary to define,
And tell those treaty makers where to draw the line.

Now the Kaiser gave his answer in 1872,
And said that Haro Strait was where the line went through.
Well they called it a war, but it wasn't very big —
And the only one got killed was a little British pig.

Old Chisholm Trail

Cowboy

Old Chisholm Trail

Oh, a ten-dollar hoss and a forty-dollar saddle,
And I'm goin' to punchin' Texas cattle.

I woke up one morning on the old Chisholm trail,
Rope in my hand and a cow by the tail.

I'm up in the mornin' afoare daylight
And afoare I sleep the moon shines bright.

Last night I was on guard and the leader broke the ranks,
I hit my horse down the shoulders and I spurred him in the flanks.

The wind commenced to blow, and the rain began to fall,
Hit looked, by grab, like we was goin' to lose 'em all.

My slicker's in the wagon and I'm gittin' mighty cold,
And these longhorn sons-o'-guns are gittin' hard to hold.

I jumped in the saddle and grabbed holt the horn,
Best blamed cow-puncher ever was born.

With my blanket and my gun and my rawhide rope,
I'm a'slidin' down the trail in a long, keen lope.

We rounded 'em up and put 'em on the cars,
And that was the last of the old Two Bars.

Oh, it's bacon and beans most every day —
I'd as soon be a'-eatin' prairie hay.

Fare you well, trail-boss, I don't wish you any harm,
I'm quittin' this business to go on the farm.

No more cow-puncher to sleep at my ease,
'Mid the crawlin' of the lice and the bitin' of the fleas.

Coma ti yi yippy, yippy yea, yippy yea,
Coma ti yi yippy, yippy yea.

Westward Ho!

Music By Tad Suckling
Words   Anonymous

I love not Col- o- ra- do Where the far- o ta- ble grows And down the des- per ra- do, The rip- pling wat- er flows; Nor seek I fair Mon- tan¯ a of bow- ie lung- ing fame; The pis- tol ring of fair Wy- o- ming I leave to nob- ler game. West-ward ho!

Westward Ho!

I love not Colorado
Where the faro table grows,
And down the desperado
The rippling water flows;

Nor seek I fair Montana
Of bowie-lunging fame;
The pistol ring of fair Wyoming
I leave to nobler game.

CHORUS

Sweet poker-haunted Kansas
In vain allures the eye;
The Nevada rough has charms enough,
Yet its blandishments I fly.

Shall Arizona woo me
Where the meek Apache bides?
Or New Mexico where natives grow
With arrow-proof insides?

BRIDGE

Nay, 'til where the grizzlies wander
And the lonely diggers roam,
And the grim Chinese from the squatter flees
That I'll make my humble home.

CHORUS

Home On The Range

Cowboy

Home On The Range

Where the air is so pure,
The zephyr so free,
The breezes so balmy and light,
That I would not exchange,
My home on the range,
For all the cities so bright.

The red man was pressed,
From this part of the West,
He's likely no more to return,
To the banks of Red River,
Where seldom, if ever,
The flickering campfires burned.

CHORUS

How often at night,
When the heavens are bright,
With the light of the glittering stars,
Have I stood here amazed,
And asked, as I gazed,
If their glory exceeds that of ours.

Oh I love these wild flowers,
And this dear land of ours,
The curlew I love to hear scream,
And I love the wide rocks,
And the antelope flocks,
That graze on the mountaintops green.

CHORUS

Oh give me a land,
Where the bright diamond sand,
Flows leisurely down the stream,
Where the graceful white swan,
Goes gliding along,
Like a maid in a heavenly dream.

Then I would not exchange,
My home on the range,
Where the deer and antelope play,
Where seldom is heard a discouraging word,
And the skies are not cloudy all day.

The Little Old Sod Shanty

Lindsey Baker
Tune: Little Log Cabin In The Lane

I am look- ing rath- er seed- y now while
hold- ing down my claim, And my
vic- tuals are not al- ways served the best; And the
mice play shy- ly round me as I nes-tle down to rest in my
lit-tle old sod shan-ty on my claim.

The Little Old Sod Shanty

The hinges are of leather and the windows have no glass,
While the board roof lets the howling blizzards in,
And I hear the hungry coyote as he slinks up through the grass
Round the little old sod shanty on my claim.

Yet, I rather like the novelty of living in this way,
Though my bill of fare is always rather tame;
But I'm as happy as a clam on the land of Uncle Sam
In the little old sod shanty on my claim.

But when I left my Eastern home, a bachelor so gay,
To try and win my way to wealth and fame,
I little thought I'd come down to burning twisted hay
In the little old sod shanty on my claim.

My clothes are plastered o'er with dough, I'm looking like a fright,
And everything is scattered round the room;
But I wouldn't give the freedom that I have out in the West
For the table of the Eastern man's own home.

Still, I wish that some kind-hearted girl would pity on me take
And relieve me from the mess that I am in;
The angel, how I'd bless her if this her home she'd make
In the little old sod shanty on my claim!

And we would make our fortunes on the prairies of the West,
Just as happy as two lovers we'd remain;
We'd forget the trials and troubles we endured at the first
In the little old sod shanty on my claim.

And if fate should bless us with now and then an heir
To cheer our hearts with honest pride of fame,
Oh, then we'd be contented for the toil that we had spent
In the little old sod shanty on our claim.

Strawberry Roan

Cowboy

I come in-to town just to spend some time, for
I had no mon-ey, not e-ven a dime. Then a
fel-low stepped up and he said, "I sup-pose you're a
bronc bust-ing cow-boy by the looks of your clothes."

Refrain

Well, it's oh, that straw-berry roan. Oh, that
straw-ber-ry roan. That straw-ber-ry po-ny no
one e-ver rode, and the cow-boy that tries it is
sure to get thrown! Oh, that straw-ber-ry roan.

Strawberry Roan

"You've guessed me just right! I'm your man," I claim.
"Do you have a wild horse you'd like me to tame?"
Well, he said that he had, and a bad one to buck,
And for throwing good riders, the horse had good luck.

REFRAIN (Two Times)

I jumped on his back and I held the reins;
That strawberry horse threw me off for my pains.
So I climbed on again to the horse's surprise,
and he tried then to throw me right up to the skies.

REFRAIN

The Old Settler

Words by Francis Henry, 1874

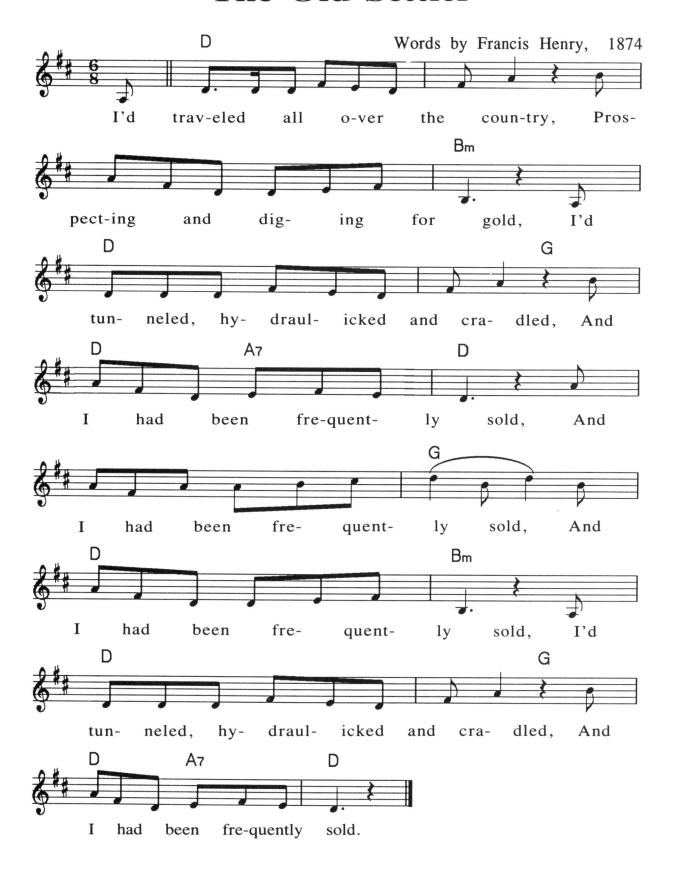

I'd trav-eled all o-ver the coun-try, Pros-

pect-ing and dig- ing for gold, I'd

tun- neled, hy- draul- icked and cra- dled, And

I had been fre-quent- ly sold, And

I had been fre- quent- ly sold, And

I had been fre- quent- ly sold, I'd

tun- neled, hy- draul- icked and cra- dled, And

I had been fre-quently sold.

The Old Settler

Where one had made riches by mining,
Perceiving that hundreds grew poor,
I made up my mind to try farming,
The only pursuit that is sure.
The only pursuit that is sure,
The only pursuit that is sure,
I made up my mind to try farming,
The only pursuit that is sure.

So, rolling my grub in my blankets,
I left all my tools on the ground,
And started one morning to shank it,
For a country they call Puget Sound.
For a country they call Puget Sound,
For a country they call Puget Sound,
And started one morning to shank it,
For a country they call Puget Sound.

Arriving flat broke in mid-winter,
I found it enveloped in fog,
and covered all over with timber,
As thick as the hair on a dog.
As thick as the hair on a dog,
As thick as the hair on a dog,
And covered all over with timber,
As thick as the hair on a dog.

I took up a claim in the forest,
And sat myself down hard to toil,
For two years I chopped and I labored,
But I never got down to the soil.
But I never got down to the soil,
But I never got down to the soil,
For two years I chopped and I labored,
But I never got down to the soil.

I tried to get out of the country,
But poverty forced me to stay,
Until I became an old settler,
Then nothing could drive me away.
Then nothing could drive me away,
Then nothing could drive me away,
Until I became an old settler,
Then nothing could drive me away.

And now that I'm used to the climate,
I think that if man ever found,
A spot to live easy and happy,
That Eden is on Puget Sound.
That Eden is on Puget Sound,
That Eden is on Puget Sound,
A spot to live easy and happy,
That Eden is on Puget Sound.

No longer the slave of ambition,
I laugh at the world and its shams,
As I think of my pleasant condition,
Surrounded by acres of clams.
Surrounded by acres of clams,
Surrounded by acres of clams,
As I think of my pleasant condition,
Surrounded by acres of clams.

The Gooey Duck Song

By Ron Konzak & J. Elfendahl

1. You can hear the dig-gers say as they're head-ed for the bay, Oh I got-ta dig a duck, got-ta dig a duck a day, 'cuz I get a buck a duck; If I dig a duck a day so I got-ta dig a duck got-ta dig a duck a day

2. Oh it takes a lot of luck and a cer-tain kind of pluck, Just dig a-round the muck just to get a goo-ey duck, Well he has-n't got a front and he has-n't got a back, he does-n't know Don-ald and does-n't go "Quack."

Dig a duck, dig a duck dig a goo-ey duck, Dig a duck dig a goo-ey duck, Dig a duck a day.

Little Cabin
(In The Cascade Mountains)

Words and Music By
Harold Weeks

Way up in the moun-tains, Man-y miles from here

There's a lit- tle cab- in that to me is dear,

Fish- in' in the sum- mer, Hunt- in' in the fall

It's a hum- mer an- y time at all —

Get up in the morn- in' feel- in' extra fine

Birds all start a sing- in' Sun be- gins to shine,

Break- fast in a hur- ry, Got a job to do

Little Cabin In The Cascade Mountains

Get my tackle ready,
String my fishing pole
Gonna catch a whopper
At my fav-'rite hole,
Stand-in' in the river,
Water all about
Flick-in flies to fool the hungry trout.

Sittin' in the even-in',
By the cabin door
Fish and bacon fryin'
Couldn't ask for more, Soon as I have eaten,
Gonna hit the hay
Proper way to end a perfect day.

CHORUS

There's a little cabin in the Cascade Mountains
That is where I long to be
Where the tall trees frown,
And the streams come tumbling down
And the trout leap lustily
Where the hills lay hazy in the sunshine
Lazy and the day ends peacefully
Oh that little cabin in the Cascade Mountains
It's a paradise to me.

Chord Chart for
Westward Ho!

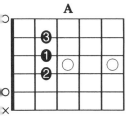 A

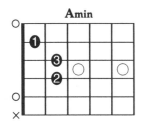 Amin

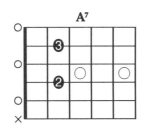 A⁷

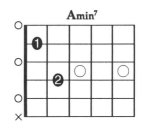 Amin⁷

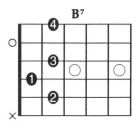 B⁷

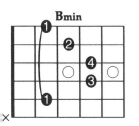 Bmin

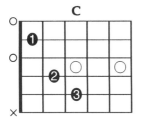 C

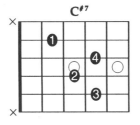 C#⁷

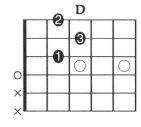 C#min

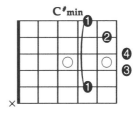 D

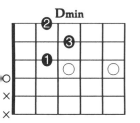 Dmin

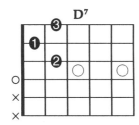 D⁷

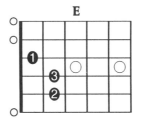 E

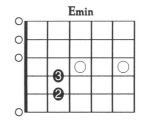 Emin

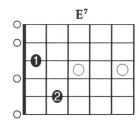 E⁷

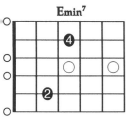 Emin⁷

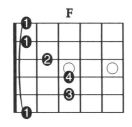 F

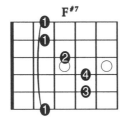 F#⁷

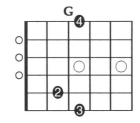 G

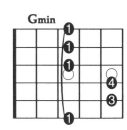 Gmin

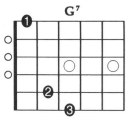 G⁷

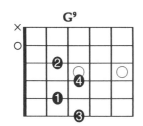 G⁹

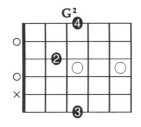 G²

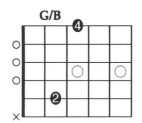 G/B

ACKNOWLEDGMENTS

APPLE PICKERS REEL
''Fort Vancouver, W.T.'' by Gustav Sohon, J. Bien N.Y. lithograph. (Public Domain)
U.S.P.R.R. Exp. & Surveys 47 & 49 Parallels.

BOLL WEEVIL
(Public Domain)

MISSIONARY'S FAREWELL
''Narcissa Whitman''
Archives: Whitman College

OH CALIFORNIA
A cartoon inspired by the California Gold Rush, suggesting various ways of reaching California. Lithograph, 1849, by Nathaniel Currier. The Granger Collection.

HO! FOR CALIFORNIA
Placer Mining, Coeur d'Alene Mines, Idaho territory, 1884. F. Jay Haynes, Photographer.
Haynes Foundation Collection, Montana Historical Society, Helena, Montana
and
Miner Panning For Gold, Colorado River, circa 1898 (No. 2095)
Seaver Center for Western History Research
Natural History Museum of Los Angeles County

SAN JUAN PIG WAR
''Guessing The Weight of A Prize Pig'' engraving, 1883.
The Bettman Archive

CHISHOLM TRAIL
''Like A Flash They Turned'' by C.M. Russell
Montana Historical Society, Mackay Collection

WESTWARD HO!
''The Rocky Mountains - Emigrants Crossing the Plains''
''Free Trapper'' by C.M. Russell, Montana Historical Society, Mackay Collection

HOME ON THE RANGE
''When The Land Belonged To God'' by C.M. Russell
Montana Historical Society, Museum Purchase

OLD SOD SHANTY
Reproduced from the Collections of the Library of Congress
No. 100755 LC-US261-127

STRAWBERRY ROAN
''Bronco Buster's Saddling'' by Fredrick Remington
The Granger Collection

OLD SETTLER
''The Pioneer'' lithograph from ''Pioneers of America'' page 730.
The Bettman Archive

GOOEY DUCK
''Geoducks On A Line''
University of Washington Libraries, Special Collections Division
Negative No.: UW 12022

LITTLE LOG CABIN IN THE CASCADE MOUNTAINS
American West: Settlements. A Log Cabin, lithograph, 1871. Negative No. 302.19.
The Granger Collection